What Is Energy?

Energy is the ability to work. When you climb a flight of stairs, your body is working and using energy.

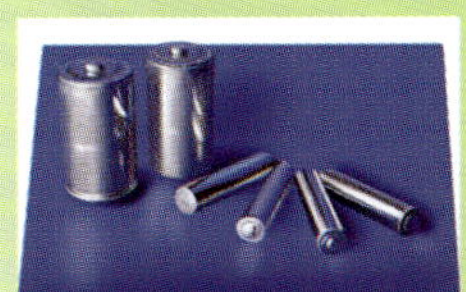

The spring inside a clockwork motor provides the energy to drive the mechanism.

A torch battery provides energy needed to light up the bulb.

The sun's energy enables plants to grow.

What is work?

To most people, 'work' means many things – sitting in an office, fixing a machine in a factory, studying in a school, mowing a lawn, washing clothes and so on. To a scientist, however, work is defined as a force that moves or changes the position of an object. This means that both 'force' and 'movement' are necessary for doing 'work'.Are you then doing any work while you are sitting? If you are writing while sitting, your hand muscles are doing work – for this they need energy.

Did you know?

The units used to measure work are named after scientists who measured work and gave a formula for it for the first time. One such unit is called the Newton after the famous British scientist, Sir Isaac Newton. Another unit, called the Joule, is named after the British physicist, James Prescott Joule, who lived between 1818 and 1889.

What is power?

Power is the rate at which something consumes or produces energy or work. A powerful car can start off and accelerate more quickly than a less powerful one. More power means spending a certain amount of energy in less time. Or, put in another way, less power means spending less energy within a certain period of time.

Remember

Power should not be confused with energy. Energy is the ability to do work. If we are to lift a weight from the ground to the waist level, we need a certain amount of energy. But the amount of power we produce depends on how quickly we lift the weight to the waist level.

Energy can have many forms

There are different kinds of energy, namely, mechanical, electrical, chemical, radiant, magnetic, heat, sound and nuclear energy. We will experiment with them in the following chapters.

Magnetic Energy

Heat Energy

Radiant Energy

Sound Energy

Mechanical Energy

EXPERIMENTS with ENERGY

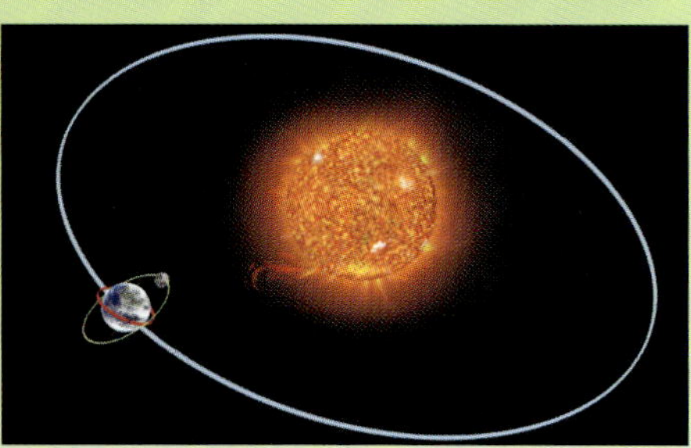

Contents

Mechanical Energy

Energy that is stored up is called 'potential energy'. Water stored behind a dam and an archer's bow drawn and ready to shoot, each has stored or potential energy. Falling water and an arrow released from a bow have moving or 'kinetic energy'. Potential and kinetic energy are forms of mechanical energy.

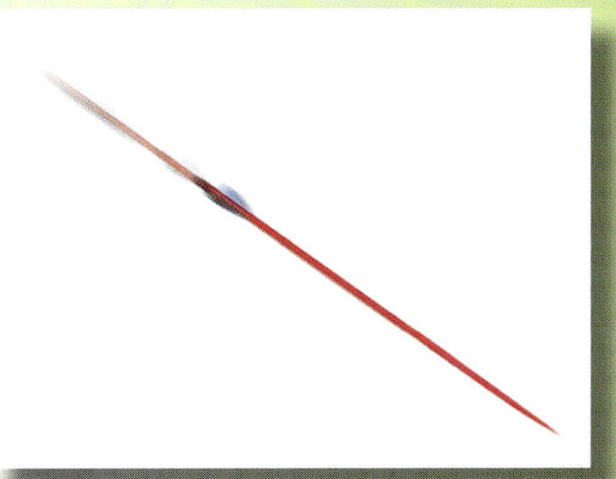

Discover the two main types of energy

You will need

- two aluminium channels of different lengths
- two steel balls or marbles
- a towel

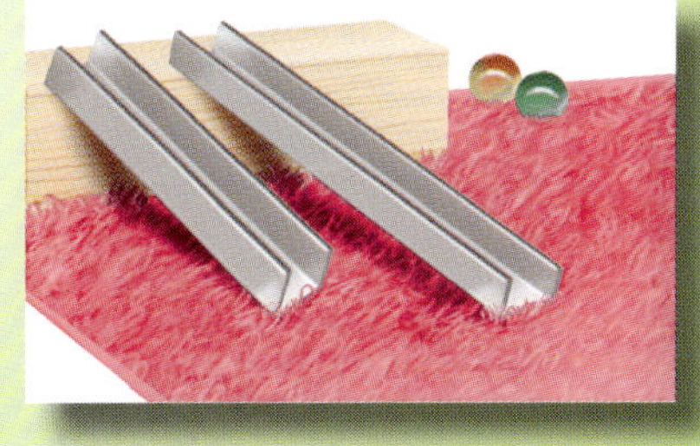

1. Spread the towel on the floor.
2. Place the two channels in such a way that their heights remain the same and they touch the floor as shown.
3. Now release the balls simultaneously from the top of the channels. They roll down and travel the same distance.

The two balls about to be released have the same potential (stored) energy because they are at the same height. As they roll down, the potential energy is gradually converted into kinetic (moving) energy.

Make your own tank

You will need:

- a thread reel
- a small elastic band
- three matchsticks
- a candle
- a ruler
- a knife

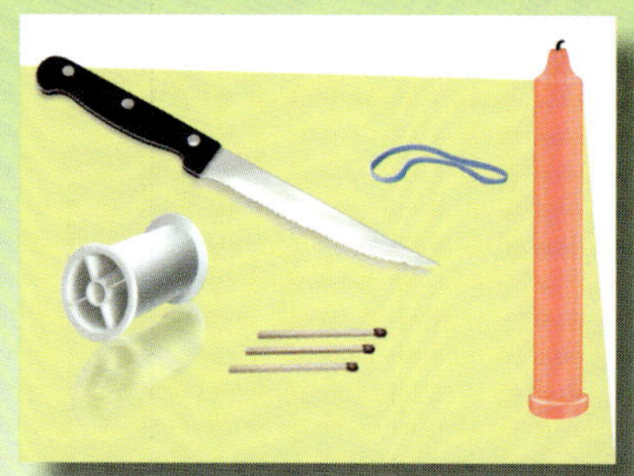

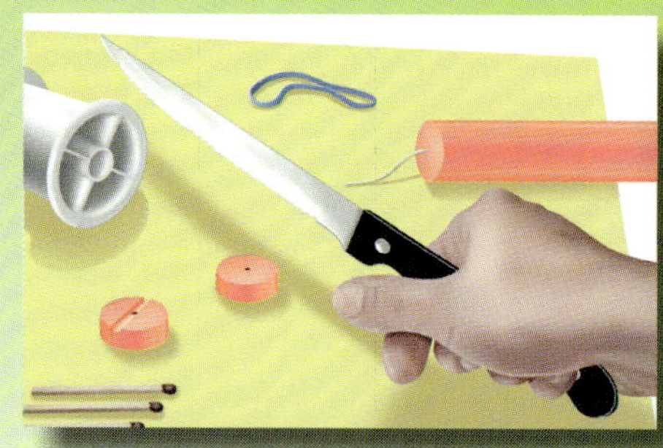

1. Cut a thin slice of wax from the candle. Widen the hole slightly in the middle of the slice. Make a groove on one side of the slice straight across the middle.
2. Push the elastic band through the hole in the slice and push a matchstick through the band. Pull the band so that the matchstick is held in the groove.
3. Pull the other end of the band through the hole in the middle of the thread reel. Push half a matchstick through the band to hold it in place.
4. Push another matchstick into one of the holes through the reel. This will stop the half matchstick from turning round.
5. To twist the elastic band, turn the matchstick in the groove several times.
6. Now put your tank on the floor or on a table and leave it. The tank will roll using the energy from the twisted elastic band.

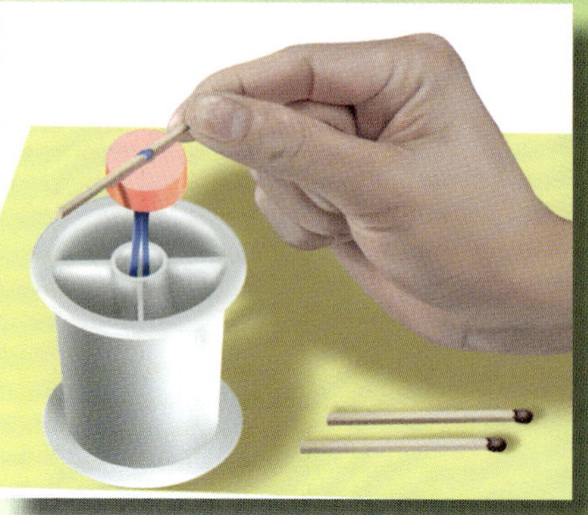

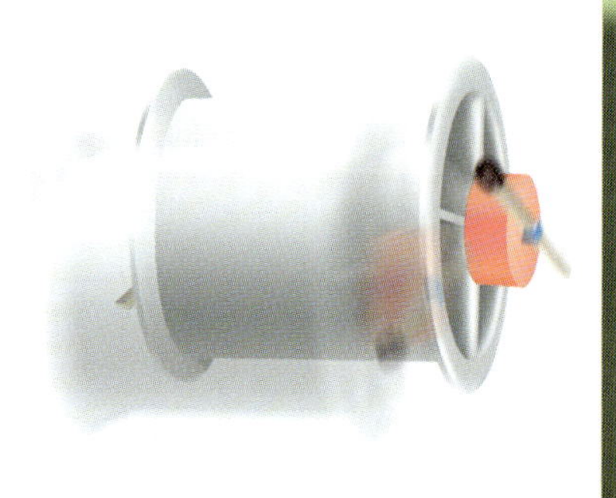

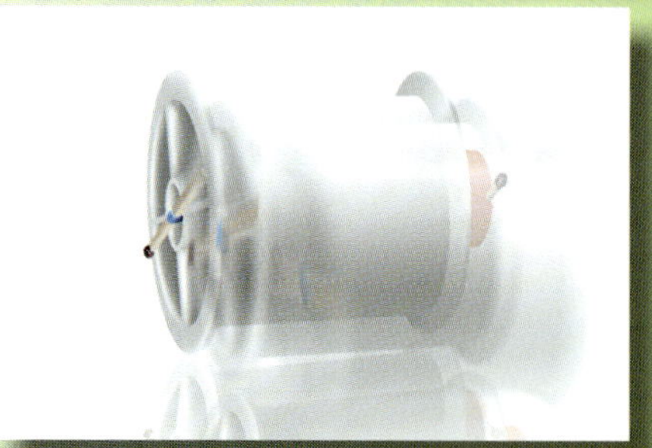

A spring toy

You will need:

- a length of wire
- a marker pen
- a cork
- a piece of paper
- tissue paper
- glue
- a pair of scissors

1. Wind the wire around the pen to make a spring. Leave an inch of straight wire at one end.
2. Push this straight end of the wire into the cork.
3. Draw a cartoon figure on the paper and cut it out. Stick the cut-out on the cork. Decorate the face with feathers cut out from the tissue paper.
4. Hold the cork between your thumb and forefinger. Now push it down on a table to squash the spring so that it stores some energy.
5. Let go of the cork. What happens?

The spring toy will leap into the air as the potential or stored energy is released as kinetic or moving energy.

Heat Energy

Heat is a form of energy we can feel but cannot see. When something burns, heat is produced.

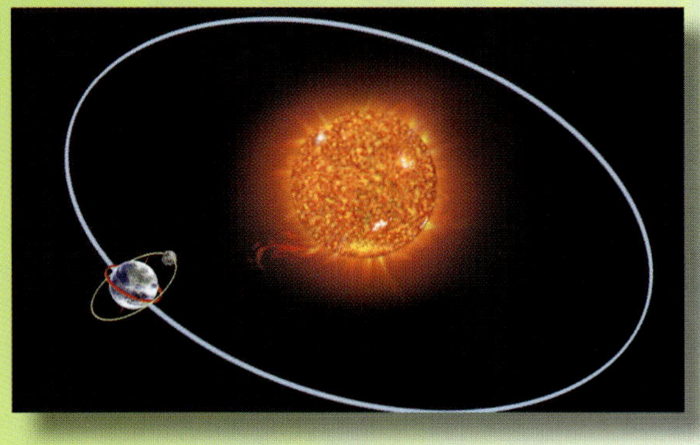

The sun gives out an enormous amount of heat. We receive just the right amount of heat from the sun so that we and our planet earth are able to survive. A few degrees less heat from the sun and our world would be a cold, lifeless waste. A few degrees more heat, and life on earth would not exist.

What gives us heat?

Most of the heat we use comes from burning fuels. Heat is also produced when electricity travels through a coil of wire. This is what makes the coil inside the toaster become red.

But heat can also be produced by 'friction', or rubbing. Can you give two examples where heat is produced by friction?

How does heat energy travel?

Heat energy travels in three ways. The heat you feel when you plug in the electric iron is carried by *conduction.* A conductor, such as iron or copper, allows heat to pass through it easily. Insulators like wood and plastic do not allow heat to pass through them.

What falls first?

You will need:

- a rod each of aluminium, brass, copper, glass and wood. They should be of the same length and thickness.
- 5 marbles
- wax
- a candle

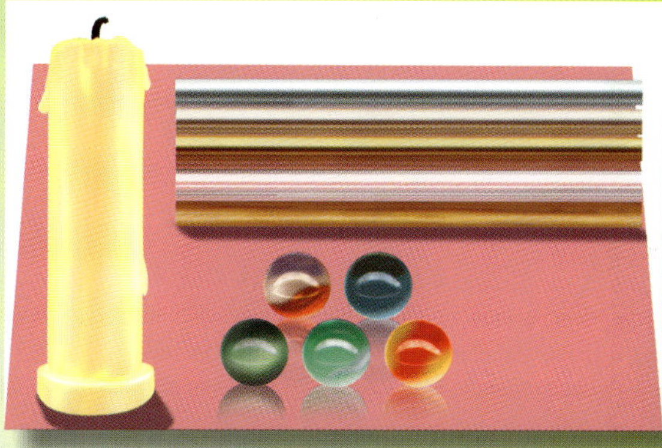

1. Stick a marble about 5 cm from the end of each rod with the help of wax. Make sure that the quantity of the wax used for sticking is the same.
2. Now heat each rod at the end at which the marble is stuck. Metals are good conductors of heat while glass and wood are not. Which of these are metal rods? Can you say this by noting the time taken by each marble to fall off?
3. You will observe that the marble on the copper rod takes the least time to fall off. Can you conclude from this that some metals are better conductors of heat than others?

The heat energy inside an electric kettle is carried by convection. Heat can travel by convection (ie, by movement of molecules from one place to another), but only in liquids and gases.

Watch the convection current

You will need:

- a coffee carafe
- water
- sawdust
- a gas burner

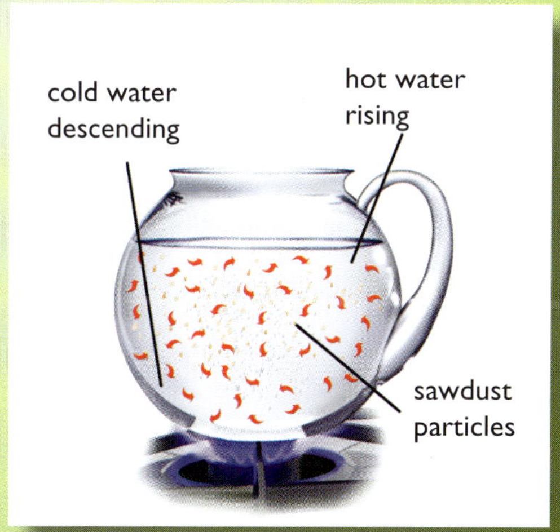

1. Fill the carafe with water and place it on low heat.
2. Put some sawdust in the water.
3. Watch the path taken by the particles of sawdust. What is this motion due to?

A whirl-fan

You will need:

- a thin circular tin disk like those used in tinned food packs
- a pair of scissors or cutters
- a knitting needle
- pliers
- a cork
- a candle
- a matchbox

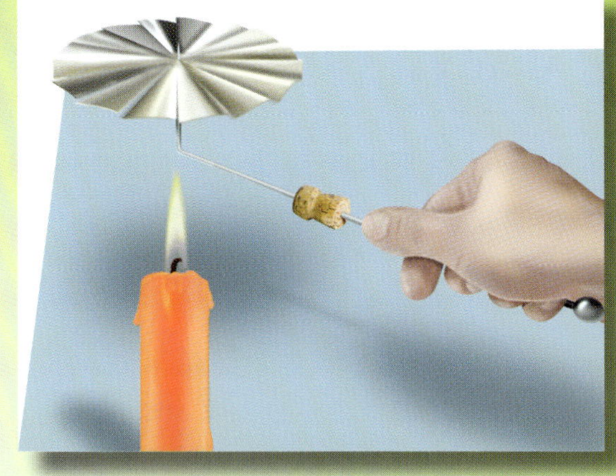

1. Cut teeth in the circumference of the tin disk.
2. Bend the teeth a little for better effects (see picture).
3. Bend the knitting needle with the pliers and push in the cork to make a handle.
4. Pivot the toothed wheel on the free end of the needle.
5. Now hold it above a candle flame and see how the wheel revolves. What do you think is turning the toothed wheel?

Heat energy from the sun travels by *radiation.* Radiation does not need any medium, like a solid, a liquid or a gas, to pass through. That is why the sun's rays penetrate the huge expanse of vacuum space before entering the earth's atmosphere.

Make fire from the sunrays

You will need:

- a magnifying glass
- a thin sheet of paper

1. In bright sunshine, place a thin piece of paper on dry ground.
2. Now focus the rays of the sun on to the sheet of paper by adjusting the position of the magnifying glass. Soon, the paper will catch fire.

Radiant Energy

Energy given out by light, radio, X-rays, infrared ultraviolet rays are examples of radiant energy. They are all various types of electromagnetic waves belonging to the electromagnetic spectrum.

What is the electromagnetic spectrum?

The electromagnetic spectrum is a band of radiation. The rays travel through space in waves of varying lengths. Light is visible and forms just one part of the spectrum. We can see only the light rays. The other parts of the spectrum are invisible to the eye. Beyond the red end of the visible light spectrum are infrared rays, microwaves, radar, television and radio waves. Beyond the other (violet) end of the spectrum are ultraviolet, X-rays, gamma rays and cosmic rays.

Try this

In which part of the spectrum is the heat energy of radiation?

Light is a form of energy similar to heat. It is the only type of energy that we can see directly. A blazing fire radiates heat and light. The heat can only be felt, but the light can be seen. Light travels in waves, much like the ripples of waves you see when you throw a pebble into a pool.

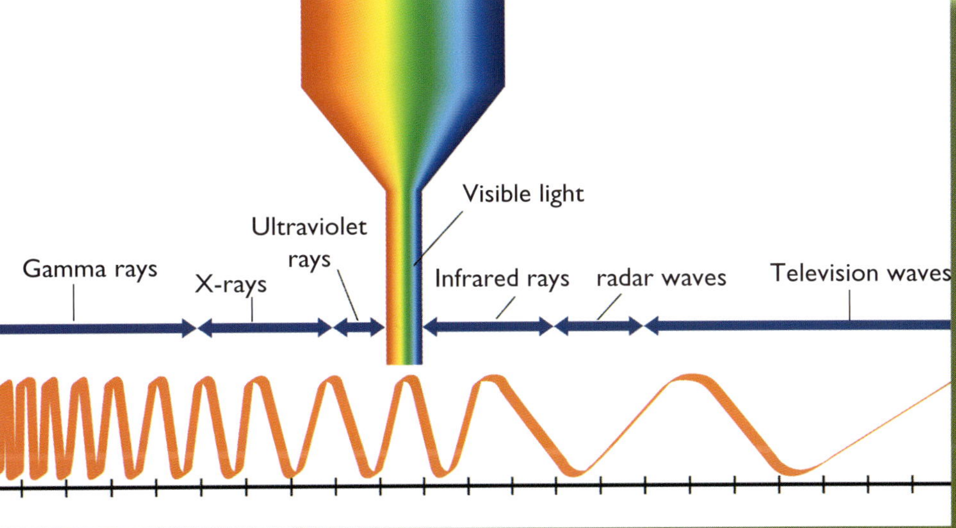

Did you know?

In 1873, the scientist, James Clerk Maxwell, discovered the wave structure of light. He showed that light is made up of vibrating waves of electrical and magnetic fields. Vibrations take place at right angles to the direction of the wave's motion, and to each other. Maxwell was the first to suggest that light was a form of 'electromagnetic radiation'. He went on to state that other kinds of rays, invisible to the eye, must also exist.

What is a photograph?

A photographic film contains chemicals which change colour when light falls on them. That means they are sensitive to light. When a camera's shutter is opened, light from the different parts of the subject is focussed by the camera lens on the exposed film. This activates the film by various degrees at different places. Thus, an image of the subject is formed.

This is later developed (treated with chemicals) to produce a photograph.

Sound Energy

Sound is also a form of energy. Unlike radiation, sound energy needs a material medium like air, water or a solid to travel through.

When does something make a sound?

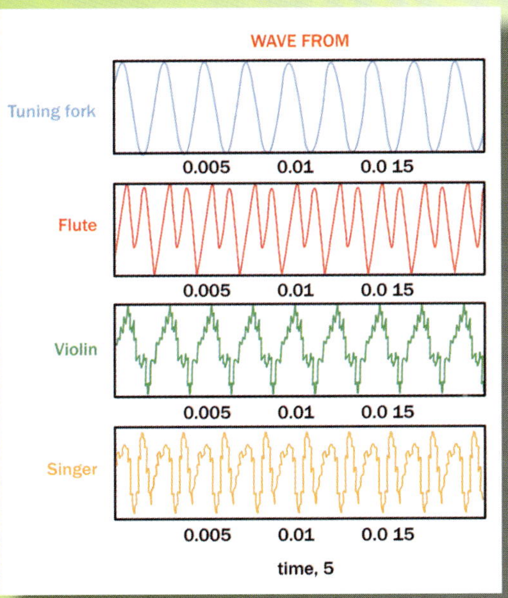

You must have noticed that nothing produces a sound unless it is struck. When a falling object, which has a lot of kinetic energy, hits the ground, three things may happen:

1. It may bounce, like a tennis ball.
2. It may change its shape, like mud.
3. Its energy may produce a lot of sound, and some heat might be produced as in a metal rod.

Most things produce a lot of waste sound energy. This is called *noise*. Some things, however, produce pleasant sounds called *music*.

Make a drum

You will need:

- an empty plastic bowl
- a plastic carry bag
- a string
- a pair of scissors
- 2 thin sticks

1. Spread out the carry bag to form a large sheet.
2. Place the plastic bowl on the sheet and cut around it keeping an extra margin of three inches.
3. With a friend's help, cover the mouth of the bowl with the plastic sheet and tie it in place. The plastic skin should be stretched as tightly as possible without any wrinkles.
4. To play the drum, beat gently with the sticks.
5. Make drums with rubber sheets, leather or hard paper, and note the difference in sound.

Wind instruments

Instruments which musicians blow into, to produce musical sounds, are called wind instruments. These instruments produce a note when the air inside them vibrates. The frequency of the vibrations depends on the length of the air column inside the instrument. The shorter the air column, the higher the pitch of the note produced.

A bottle organ

You will need:

- 8 bottles of the same type
- water

1. Fill water in the bottles up to different levels (see picture).
2. Blow across each bottle in turn. You will notice that the higher the water level, the higher the pitch of the notes.
3. Adjust the water levels in the bottles to get a musical scale.

Chemical Energy

Energy stored up in molecules of chemicals that are released when one chemical reacts with another, is called chemical energy. Molecules of food or fossil fuels such as coal and oil are specially rich in chemical energy. Fuels are substances that give off heat when they burn by reacting with oxygen in the air. Fuels provide us with energy that we use for heating, cooking, powering ships, planes, cars and machines, and for producing electricity. For example, we say that coal is a source of energy. When coal burns, it forms new chemicals. The energy stored in coal gets converted into heat. Heat produced from coal can be used to make steam which drives a steam engine.

Photosynthesis

The process by which green plants turn carbon dioxide and water into food using energy from sunlight is known as photosynthesis. Hence, the sunlight is necessary for plants to grow. Plants are consumed by animals and human beings. This gives us energy to do work.

Try this

Choose a healthy green plant with big leaves. Cover one leaf with two pieces of cardboard, one from the top and the other from the bottom. Clip the cardboard pieces together and leave it for 2-3 days. Now remove the cardboard pieces. What change do you notice in the leaves?

Electrical Energy

Electricity is a form of energy which is produced by the movement or flow of electrons. Electrons are extremely tiny particles present in the atoms of all elements. The energy released by the movement of electrons may be large, as in a flash of lightning, or small, as in the glow of a torch.

Electricity can be of two types, *static electricity,* if it is localised and *current electricity,* if it is flowing.

Feel the static power

1. Rub a plastic comb on a piece of woollen cloth. It will become charged with static electricity.
2. Now take the comb close to some tiny bits of paper. What happens? What do you think, is attracting the bits of paper to the comb?
3. Hold the same charged comb close to a thin stream of water running from a tap. The water will bend towards the comb.

Sticky balloons

1. Rub a few inflated balloons several times on a piece of woollen cloth.
2. Now hold them against a wall. The strong static charge on the balloons will make them cling to the wall as if they are glued there.

Make your own lightning

Lightning is a kind of static electricity.

You will need:

- a large iron or steel saucepan with a plastic handle
- a pair of rubber gloves
- an iron or steel fork
- a plastic sheet
- sellotape

1. Tape the plastic sheet on to a table top.
2. Hold the saucepan by its handle with a gloved hand. Rub the pan vigorously to and fro on the plastic sheet. This gives electrical charge to the pan.
3. Now, hold a fork firmly in the other hand. Bring its prongs slowly near the saucepan's rim. When the gap between the pan and the fork is very narrow, a tiny spark will jump across. You will get better results if you conduct your experiment in a darkened room.

Electric current

Electric current is produced by batteries and electric generators.
There are special chemicals inside a battery. The battery works until all the chemicals have changed into other chemicals.

Make a battery

You will need:

- clean, shiny one-rupee coins
- blotting paper
- salt
- an aluminium foil
- 2 thin insulated wires
- a low-watt bulb

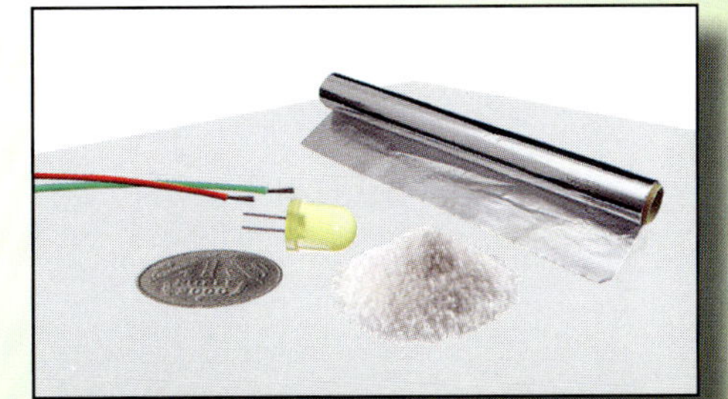

1. Cut up the foil and blotting paper into many small squares. Soak the squares of blotting paper in salty water.
2. Make a pile of coins, foil and salty blotting paper, keeping the layers in this order. The bigger the pile, the more powerful the battery.
3. Cut off 2 cm off the insulated plastic, covering the ends of each wire. Put one end of a wire underneath the pile. Connect the other wire to the top of the pile.
4. To test your battery, join the free ends of the two wires to the bulb. Does the bulb light up? What does this show?

An electric generator has to be powered by a fuel such as coal or oil to produce an electric current. It contains magnets and coils of wire that turn and produce electricity.

Generate electricity at home

You will need:

- a flexible iron rod (15 cm x 1 cm x 3 mm)
- some copper wire
- a bar magnet (8 cm x 1 cm x 5 mm)
- 2 wooden reels with thread wound on them
- a knitting needle
- an iron strip
- screws
- a wooden plank
- a bulb (1.5 watts)
- pliers

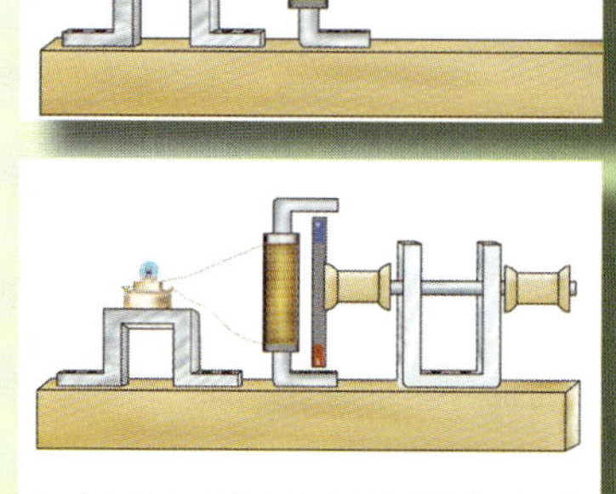

1. Bend the ends of the iron rod with pliers, as shown.
2. Now wind five layers of insulated copper wire on it.
3. Connect both ends of the wire to a bulb.
4. Fix the bar magnet on one side of a wooden reel.
5. Connect this reel to another reel with the help of a knitting needle. For support, pass this knitting needle through an iron strip (first, you will have to drill holes in it). Fix the reels such that the reel with the magnet comes on the side of the coiled wire.
6. Secure the entire apparatus with screws on a wooden plank, as shown.
7. Now connect the second reel with thread to a cycle wheel.
8. Set the wheel in motion. The first as well as the second wheel start rotating because of the thread's pressure. The bar magnet too starts rotating and an electric current starts flowing through the coil. This makes the bulb light up. If you increase the speed of the wheel, the bulb will glow brighter.

Power station generators are developed on the same principle. The power of the electric current depends on three things the number of turns in the coil, the power of the rotating magnet and its speed.

Magnetic Energy

Some materials called magnets have the peculiar property of attracting iron and attracting or repelling other magnets when brought closer to each other. The energy possessed by magnets is called magnetic energy.

Make your own magnet

You will need:

- a steel needle
- a bar magnet
- paper clips

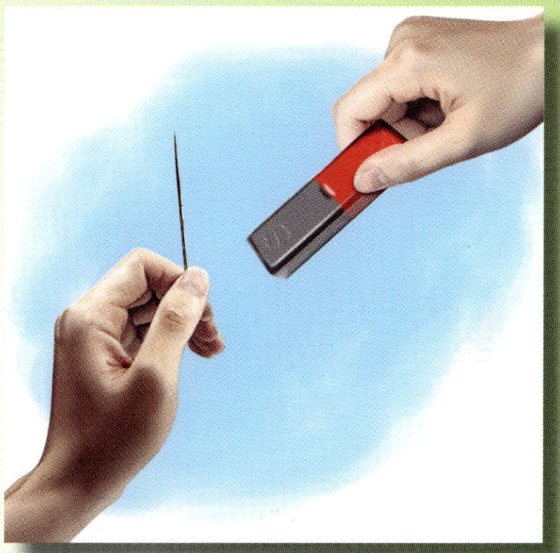

1. Hold the steel needle near the paper clips. Do they stick to the needle? Be sure that the needle is not magnetised.
2. Hold the needle in one hand and the magnet in the other. Stroke the needle with the north pole of the magnet, starting from the middle and moving to the eye of the needle.
3. Repeat this 20-30 times. Always stroke in one direction. Do not drag the magnet back and forth.
4. Use the south pole of the magnet and stroke the other end of the needle in the same way.
5. Touch the paper clips with the needle. What happens?
6. Bring the eye of the needle near the south pole of the bar magnet. What do you notice? Repeat this with the north pole. Do you know the poles of your magnetised needle? Mark them.

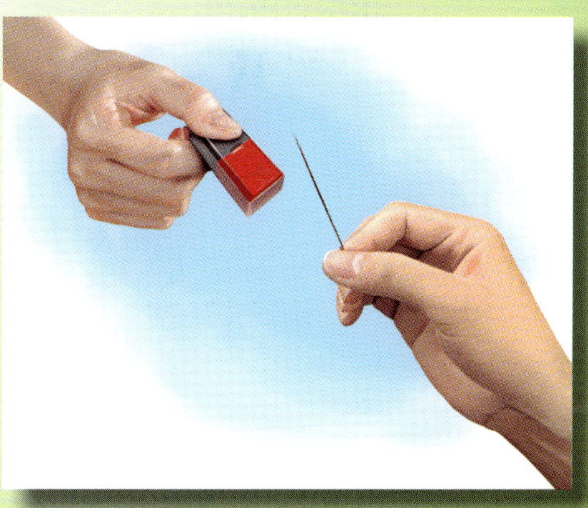

A floating doll

It is an anti-gravity equipment.

You will need:

- a bar magnet
- a paper clip
- coloured paper
- a pair of scissors
- thread
- sellotape

1. Make a tiny paper doll and fix it to the paper clip.
2. Tie one end of a 5 inch piece of thread to the doll. Tape the other end of the thread to the table.
3. Slowly bring the magnet closer to the doll and raise it. You are not allowed to touch it. Make the doll stand up. How long can you make her float?

Make an electromagnet

You can make an electric-current magnet using a length of copper wire and a large nail.

1. Wind the wire around the nail several times and tape it in place.
2. Join the ends of the wire to the two terminals of a battery through a switch.
3. Press the switch and bring some paper clips and pins near the nail. Watch them jump on to the nail!

Nuclear Energy

Nuclear energy, or energy stored in an atom, is the most powerful energy source we know on earth.

All materials are made up of tiny building blocks called *atoms*. Each atom has a nucleus in the centre. The nucleus is made up of neutron and proton particles. The nucleus is surrounded by particles called *electrons*.

Some atoms give off streams of particles called *radiation*. These atoms can be split into two (a process called fission). In nuclear power stations, radioactive nuclei are bombarded with neutrons, until they split apart.

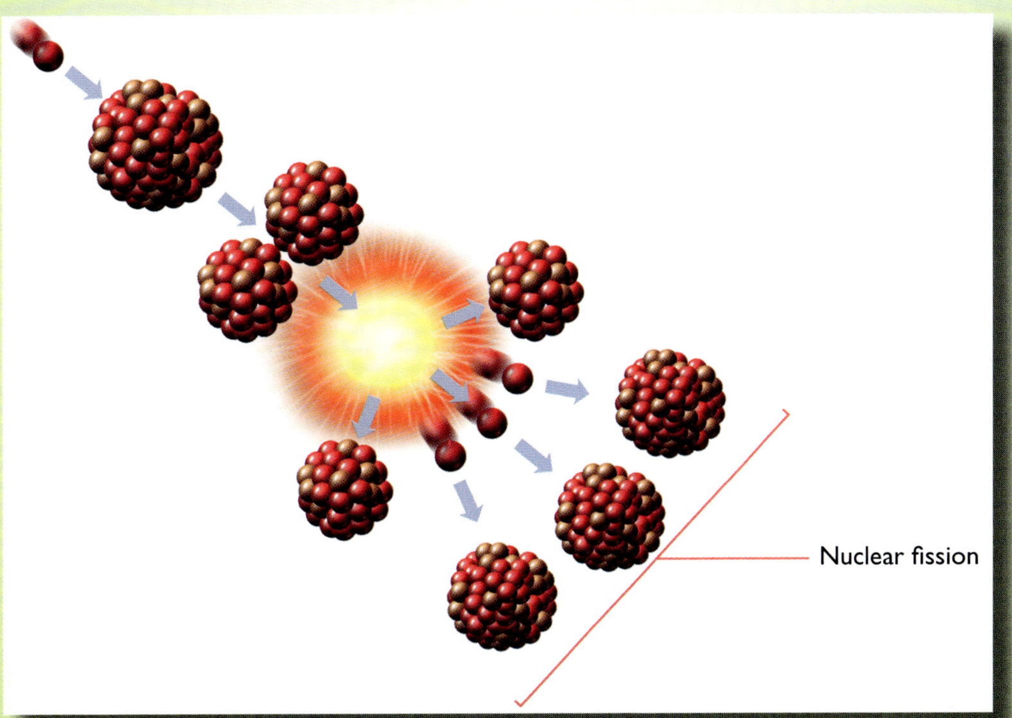

Fission gives off large amounts of heat. In a nuclear power station, fission is controlled so that it gives enough heat to boil water. The steam from the boiling water is then used to drive an electricity-producing turbine. You can see the process above.

Conservation of Energy

By now, you know that when you lift a hammer to hit a nail, the raised hammer gains potential energy. As the hammer hits the nail, that energy is made to do work. The nail is thus driven into the wood. Potential or stored energy has been changed into kinetic energy, or energy of motion. Similarly, heat energy can be changed into electrical energy, electrical energy can become radiant energy (such as light), chemical energy can become mechanical energy, and so on and so forth. In other words, we may say that energy can change from one form to another. It can neither be created nor destroyed. That is, the total energy is always conserved.

Try this

How many examples of energy conversion can you give from your daily life? Where does all the energy that you spend but cannot feel being converted into other forms, go?

See energy in action

You will need:

- an empty injection vial
- two matchsticks
- a magnifying glass

1. Take an empty injection vial with its rubber cap.
2. Place the matchstick inside the vial. Ensure that inflammable end of the matchstick is towards the bottom of the vial.
3. Now wet the rubber cap and place it on the mouth of the vial, but not too tightly.

4. Keep the vial in the sun.
5. With the magnifying glass, focus the sun's rays on the inflammable material inside the vial.

The inflammable material will soon catch fire and the rubber cap will be blown off. How many energy changes did you observe in the process?

This is the principle at work in a motor car. The only difference is that instead of the inflammable material, there is a thin jet of petrol. For ignition, a spark plug is used instead of a magnifying glass.

Feel the heat

You will need:

- two battery cells
- a bulb (1.5 watts) with a holder
- two paper clips
- two pieces of insulating wire

1. Fix the bulb firmly in the bulb holder.
2. Clip one end of a wire to the positive terminal of the battery and fix the other end of the wire to one side of the bulb holder.
3. Join one end of the second wire to the negative terminal and the other end to the bulb holder.
4. The bulb will light up. Now feel the bulb. It is warm. The chemical in the battery produced electricity, which passed through the wire and made the bulb glow as well as produce heat.

The human body uses energy too

We need fuel to keep our body warm. This fuel is the food we eat. The human body contains a surprising amount of heat. The heat it produces is about the same as the heat produced by a 120-watt electric bulb! You can see, therefore, why it can become quite hot if a lot of people are gathered in a room.

Make a model of an energy cycle

Apply your creativity using paper, wool and other materials to make the following energy cycle. You can make your own charts too.

1. Light from the sun makes trees grow (light energy to chemical energy).
2. Over millions of years, the trees turn into coal (chemical energy).
3. The coal is used as fuel in power stations (chemical to heat energy).
4. The burning coal heats water to produce steam which drives a turbine (heat to kinetic energy).
5. The turbine rotates to produce electricity (kinetic to electrical energy).
6. The current reaches home to light bulbs (electrical to light energy).

A Thermoelectric Power Station

Sources of Energy

The ultimate source of almost all forms of energy is the energy that comes from the sun by radiation. This energy is converted by plants into substances which enable them to grow until they are consumed by animals. All our chemical fuels, like wood, coal, oil and natural gas, are derived from plants and animals which are ultimately dependent on the sun.

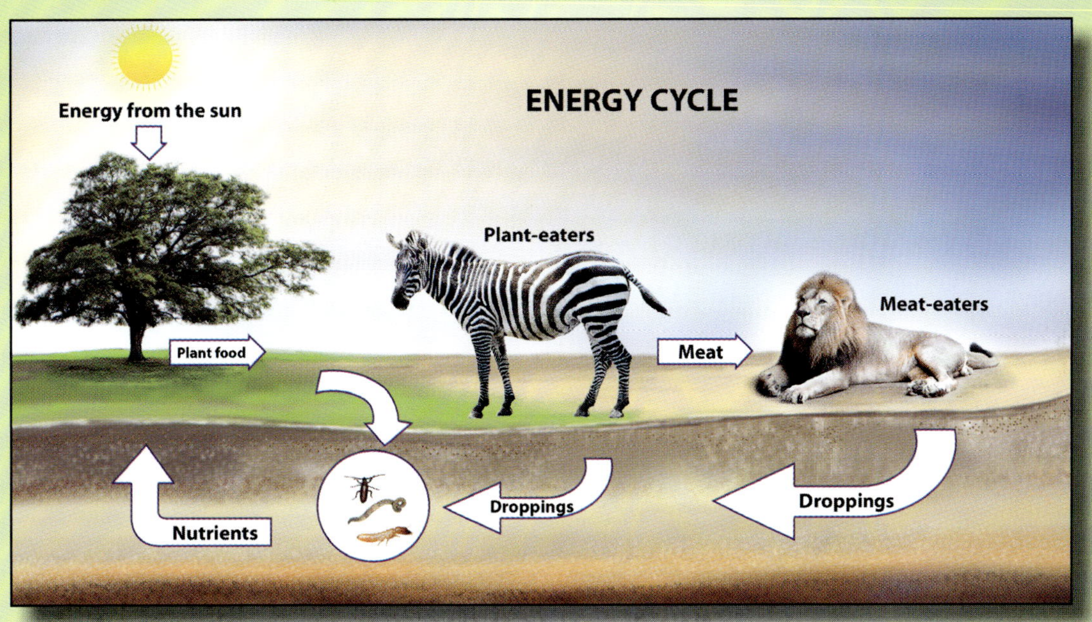

Fuel

Coal is one of the most important sources of energy. It is a fossil fuel found in layers, or seams, under the ground. It is used for heating purposes as fuel for boilers and steam engines, and for the generation of electricity by thermal power plants.

Another important fossil fuel is *mineral oil.* It is found trapped under rocks. Engineers drill holes down through layers of rocks to reach the oil beneath. It gushes up or can be pumped up to the surface.

Oil refineries separate the oil to make petrol, paraffin and lubricating oil. When petroleum is burned, heat is released.

The gas we use in cooking, heating our homes, and running machines in factories is called *natural gas*. It is also an important fuel too.

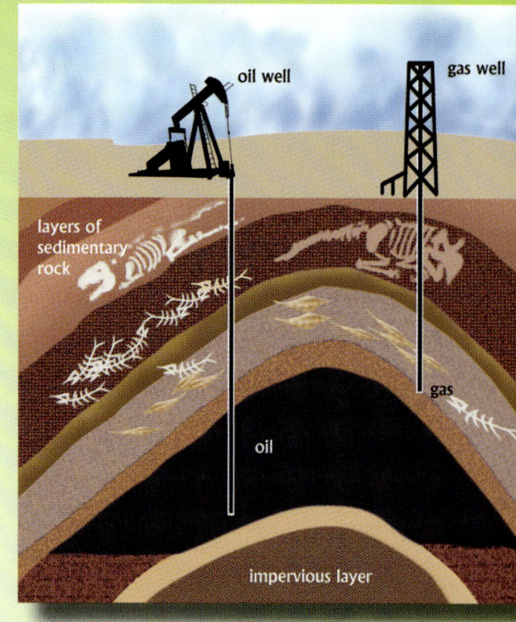

Hydro energy

Rain and snow feed rivers and lakes. This water can be stored behind dams and released in a controlled way to generate hydro power. The potential energy of water stored at a height is converted into mechanical and electrical energy as this water falls and drives turbines and electric generators. Hydro energy can also be tapped from flowing and falling waterfalls. About a quarter of the world's electricity comes from hydro power.

Make a water wheel

You will need:

- an empty plastic bottle
- two corks
- small pieces of plastic or wood
- a knitting needle
- a pair of scissors
- thread
- an empty matchbox

1. Cut four plastic or wooden fins.
2. Make four slits in the sides of the cork, and one hole through the middle of the cork.

3. Push the fins into the slits in the cork.
4. Make a hole at the bottom of the plastic bottle.
5. Push the knitting needle through the cork with the fins into the bottle and out through the hole at the bottom.
6. Now push the point of the knitting needle into the other cork. The needle should be able to turn round inside the cork.
7. Hold the bottle and put your water wheel under a tap and watch it turn round.
8. Tie a long thread with a matchbox on the other end to the second cork. As the water wheel turns, it will lift up the matchbox.

Alternate sources of energy

Natural sources or fossil fuels such as gas and oil will eventually run out, so scientists are searching for new and alternate forms of energy.

Wind

Wind is an important source of energy and can be used to generate electricity. Wind energy is not a new idea. For centuries, it has been used to power windmills for grinding corn and lifting water.
The blades of a modern windmill are connected to a wind turbine. When the turbine turns, it powers a generator. A flip side of such a generator is that, it works only when the wind blows.

Make a windmill

You will need:

- a piece of coloured paper about 15 sq cm
- a pair of scissors
- a pin
- a bead
- a stick

1. Cut lines on the piece of paper to match the picture.
2. Fold in the pieces marked with a cross.
3. Push the pin through the middle of the folded pieces.
4. Thread the bead on to the back of the pin. Now push the pin into a stick.
5. When there is wind put your windmill outside and see how fast it turns.

Solar energy

Solar energy comes from sunlight. It can be converted into electricity by solar cells. These can be used for everyday items such as watches, calculators and transisters.

Solar energy is collected through solar panels which may be used to cook food and heat houses.

Tidal energy

The sea is a valuable source of energy. The movements of tides and waves are being harnessed to generate electricity.

Geothermal energy

An enormous store of energy lies beneath the earth's surface. Some deep layers of rock in the earth's crust are very hot, while the temperature at the centre of the earth is believed to be 6,000°C. Energy from beneath the earth's surface is called *'geothermal' energy*. Geysers are a well-known source of geothermal energy.

Bio-energy

All biological forms of matter such as plants, vegetables, enzymes, human and animal wastes, provide the basis for energy or its conversion from one form to another. The widest use of bio-energy is the traditional way where wood, plants and other agricultural matterials are directly burnt to provide heat. *Biogas* obtained from organic materials like cattle dung, human wastes and other different types of biomass is a clean and smokeless domestic fuel.